T0403213

AUSTRALIA

by Samantha S. Bell

FOCUS READERS®
NAVIGATOR

Focus Readers is distributed by North Star Editions:
sales@northstareditions.com | 888-417-0195

Produced for Focus Readers by Red Line Editorial.

Content Consultant: Timothy Rowse, PhD, Emeritus Professor, Institute for Culture and Society, Western Sydney University

Photographs ©: iStockphoto, cover, 1; Shutterstock Images, 4–5, 8–9, 11, 14–15, 16, 19, 20–21, 23, 25, 26–27; Red Line Editorial, 7; AP Images, 13; Rick Rycroft/AP Images, 28

Library of Congress Cataloging-in-Publication Data
Names: Bell, Samantha, author.
Title: Australia / by Samantha S. Bell.
Description: Mendota Heights, MN: Focus Readers, [2025] | Series:
 Countries | Includes index. | Audience: Grades 4-6
Identifiers: LCCN 2024023645 (print) | LCCN 2024023646 (ebook) | ISBN
 9798889982173 (hardcover) | ISBN 9798889982739 (paperback) | ISBN
 9798889983798 (pdf) | ISBN 9798889983293 (ebook)
Subjects: LCSH: Australia--Juvenile literature.
Classification: LCC DU96 .B45 2025 (print) | LCC DU96 (ebook) | DDC
 994--dc23/eng/20240531
LC record available at https://lccn.loc.gov/2024023645
LC ebook record available at https://lccn.loc.gov/2024023646

Printed in the United States of America
Mankato, MN
012025

ABOUT THE AUTHOR

Samantha S. Bell lives in the foothills of the Blue Ridge Mountains with her family and lots of cats. She is the author of more than 150 nonfiction books for kids from kindergarten through high school. She loves learning about the different countries and cultures that are part of our amazing world.

TABLE OF CONTENTS

CHAPTER 1

WELCOME TO AUSTRALIA

Australia is a country in the southern hemisphere. It is located between the Indian Ocean and the Pacific Ocean. Australia is made up of six states. It also includes two **territories**. The country's capital is Canberra.

Most Australians live on the east coast. The three biggest cities are there.

More than 8,200 islands, including the Whitsunday Islands, are part of Australia.

These cities are Sydney, Melbourne, and Brisbane. Perth is the fourth biggest city. It is on the west coast.

Australia has a wide variety of landscapes. Some areas are mountainous. The Great Dividing Range is Australia's longest and highest mountain range. It is in the east. The longest river in Australia is the Murray River. It flows west and then south into the Southern Ocean. The river helps form the Murray-Darling **Basin**.

Much of the middle of Australia is very dry. The land is covered in sandy deserts and coarse grasses. These regions are known as the Outback. Fewer people live in the Outback than any other region.

Australia is full of people from many different backgrounds. The country's cultures, landscapes, and wildlife make it a fascinating place.

MAP OF AUSTRALIA

INDIAN OCEAN

Torres Strait

Darwin

NORTHERN TERRITORY

The Outback

AUSTRALIA

Uluru

WESTERN AUSTRALIA

Great Barrier Reef

PACIFIC OCEAN

QUEENSLAND

The Outback

Great Dividing Range

Brisbane

Perth

SOUTH AUSTRALIA

NEW SOUTH WALES

Murray-Darling Basin

Adelaide

Canberra

Sydney

AUSTRALIAN CAPITAL TERRITORY

Murray River

VICTORIA

N W E S

SOUTHERN OCEAN

Melbourne

TASMANIA

Hobart

CHAPTER 2

HISTORY

Humans have lived in Australia for approximately 60,000 years. Many early **Aboriginal** people lived on Australia's mainland. Other groups lived on islands in the Torres Strait. These groups are called the Torres Strait Islander peoples. All these native groups are known as the First Nations.

The Torres Strait is a body of water between New Guinea and Australia's mainland.

Different early groups had their own languages and territories. But the societies also had similarities. They shared some beliefs and practices. Most of these early cultures were mobile. They moved from place to place.

In 1606, a Dutch explorer sailed to the continent. He wanted to find gold and other resources. Later, other outsiders came. In the 1700s, prisons in Great Britain were getting too full. So, the government sent prisoners to Australia. In 1788, the first prison ships arrived in Port Jackson. Prison settlements became the first European **colonies** in Australia. Later, Britain let free people settle there.

A prison site at Port Arthur in Tasmania became a museum. Visitors can learn about the area's history.

Settlers brought millions of sheep. They grew wool to sell back to Britain.

In 1851, people found gold in New South Wales. The discovery brought a new wave of settlers. Hundreds of thousands of people came from all over the world. They hoped to get rich.

White settlers harmed First Nations people. Settlers took the land. They forced native people into smaller areas.

Settlers also killed thousands of native people. Their actions wiped out many First Nations cultural traditions.

During the 1800s, British colonists formed six colonies. Each had its own laws and taxes. By the end of the century, many people believed the colonies should join together. Leaders from each

CREATING A NAME

For many years, Europeans knew little about the continent. They called it *Terra Australis Incognita*. That means "Unknown Southern Land" in Latin. In 1803, an English explorer sailed around the continent. He created a map. On the map, he shortened the Latin phrase. He wrote *Australia*.

Australia hosted the Olympics in 1956. Melbourne was the host city.

colony met. In 1901, they formed the Commonwealth of Australia.

At first, the Australian government only controlled matters inside the country. The British government controlled foreign affairs. Over the next 40 years, that changed. Australia grew into the modern nation of today.

CHAPTER 3

CLIMATE, PLANTS, AND ANIMALS

The climate varies across Australia. Desert regions are extremely hot. Temperatures often reach above 100 degrees Fahrenheit (38°C). Colder regions can drop below freezing. The northern areas are typically warmer and more humid. Southern areas are colder. It rains most in dense rainforests.

Huge birds called emus live in Australia. These birds cannot fly, but they run fast.

Koalas live in eastern and southeastern Australia. They eat the leaves of eucalyptus trees.

Australia is home to many unusual native animals. For example, only two **mammals** in the world lay eggs. They are the platypus and the echidna. Both live in Australia. Koalas and emus are found in Australia, too. The country's most dangerous animal is the saltwater crocodile. Australia also has many kangaroos. In fact, the country has twice as many kangaroos as people.

Gum trees and tea trees are common in Australia. Many landscapes also feature golden wattle. That is Australia's national tree. In Australia's desert areas, fewer plants can survive. The most common plants there are acacia trees.

THE GREAT BARRIER REEF

The Great Barrier Reef is off Australia's northeast coast. It covers approximately 134,000 square miles (347,000 sq km). The reef has amazing **biodiversity**. More than 1,500 types of fish and 400 types of coral live there. Large animals such as sea turtles, sharks, and whales live by the Great Barrier Reef, too.

RISING HEAT

Climate change is harming Australia in many ways. Bushfires are a common part of summer. But higher temperatures are making these fires stronger. Fire seasons are lasting longer, too. In the early 2020s, some fires burned for nine months. Rainfall plays a role, too. Some areas get less rain than before. That makes the fires worse. In contrast, some areas are getting more rain. That causes damaging floods.

Climate change also threatens other parts of nature. In the Great Barrier Reef, high water temperature harms the corals. The heat makes corals lose their algae. The corals turn white. This process is called coral bleaching. Corals often die after bleaching. Coral death causes a chain reaction. It harms the whole **ecosystem**. Fish and other animals can't get what they need to survive.

Bushfires may destroy the habitats of wildlife such as kangaroos.

Climate change also impacts Australia's people. High temperatures cause heat waves. These periods of hot weather can last several days. Sometimes people die from the heat. In fact, since 1900, heat waves have caused more deaths in Australia than all other natural disasters.

CHAPTER 4

RESOURCES, ECONOMY, AND GOVERNMENT

Australia has a wide variety of natural resources. People mine materials in many areas of the country. Common materials include aluminum ore and iron ore. People use them to make metal products. In other areas, miners dig for uranium. They also dig for gold and diamonds.

The Super Pit is the largest open-pit gold mine in Australia.

Australia is a large producer of energy sources, too. These include natural gas and coal. Both are major exports. Australia sells them to other countries.

Agriculture is also a key part of Australia's economy. Many farmers raise cows. The cows are used for dairy and beef. Most cows are raised in warm northern areas. In the south, farmers tend to grow crops. The country's hot, dry interior has many grasslands. These areas are great for raising sheep. Like early settlers, modern Australians still use sheep to produce wool.

Tourism is another of Australia's biggest industries. People come to see

Tourists can travel 150 miles (240 km) along the Great Ocean Road in Victoria.

sites all over the country. Each year, millions of tourists visit the Great Barrier Reef. They go snorkeling, fishing, and boating. The Sydney Harbour Bridge is popular, too. Visitors can climb to the top of it. They view the city and its harbor.

Many tourists also travel to see Uluru. This giant red rock is in the Northern Territory.

Australia is still connected to the British government. The British king is the **symbolic** head of Australia. An official in the Australian government represents him. However, Australia has its own national government.

Australia's government includes three branches. The executive branch has the prime minister. This person is the leader of the government. The legislative branch makes laws for the country. The group of lawmakers is called Parliament. Australian people vote to choose

Lawmakers meet at Parliament House in Canberra.

members of Parliament. And members of Parliament vote for the prime minister. The third branch is the judicial branch. This branch includes the country's judges and courts. They help decide what the laws mean. States and territories have governments, too. Each one has its own leaders, lawmakers, and judges.

CHAPTER 5

PEOPLE AND CULTURE

More than 26 million people live in Australia. The population is **diverse**. People speak more than 300 languages across the country. English is the most common language. Many other languages come from First Nations. Mandarin and Arabic are also common languages in some areas.

Sydney is one of Australia's most famous cities. More than five million people live there.

Members of First Nations groups march for International Day of the World's Indigenous Peoples in Sydney.

At first, Australia allowed only white people to come. But since the 1970s, Australia has welcomed people from many continents. Many come from Asian countries.

First Nations people are still an important part of Australia's population. Approximately one million Aboriginal and Torres Strait Islander people live in the country. In the past, white settlers killed or jailed many. Today, First Nations people still deal with the effects of these actions. Their communities deal with worse education and health. But their cultural impact is strong. They add to modern Australia's diverse culture and society.

HAVING FUN IN AUSTRALIA

Australia is famous for fun outdoor activities. That includes many water activities. Australian beaches are great for swimming. Some people visit the beach every day. The waters are also great for surfing. Surfing is a popular hobby in the country.

FOCUS QUESTIONS

Write your answers on a separate piece of paper.

1. Write a few sentences describing the main ideas of Chapter 4.

2. What part of Australia's history do you find the most interesting? Why?

3. What animal did settlers bring to Australia?
   - **A.** sheep
   - **B.** koalas
   - **C.** kangaroos

4. What will happen if all the coral in the Great Barrier Reef becomes bleached?
   - **A.** The reef will grow much bigger.
   - **B.** More types of coral will live there.
   - **C.** Many animals will lose their habitats.

Answer key on page 32.

GLOSSARY

Aboriginal
Native to Australia, or belonging to ancestors who lived in Australia since before European arrival.

basin
An area of land where smaller bodies of water drain into the same larger body of water.

biodiversity
The number of different species that live in an area.

climate change
A human-caused global crisis involving long-term changes in Earth's temperature and weather patterns.

colonies
Areas controlled by a country that is far away.

diverse
Having a lot of variety.

ecosystem
The collection of living things in a natural area.

mammals
Animals that have hair and produce milk for their young.

symbolic
Holding a position without having much power.

territories
Areas under government control that are not states.

TO LEARN MORE

BOOKS

Doeden, Matt. *Travel to Australia.* Minneapolis: Lerner Publications, 2022.

Hamby, Rachel. *Restoring the Great Barrier Reef.* Mendota Heights, MN: Focus Readers, 2020.

Reynolds, A. M. *Your Passport to Australia.* North Mankato, MN: Capstone Press, 2022.

NOTE TO EDUCATORS

Visit **www.focusreaders.com** to find lesson plans, activities, links, and other resources related to this title.

INDEX